STUDYING WEATHER

WEATHER REPORT

Ted O'Hare

Rourke
Publishing LLC
Vero Beach, Florida 32964

www.rourkepublishing.com

PHOTO CREDITS: NASA, cover, title page, pages 8, 15; courtesy South Dakota Tourism, page 12; courtesy University of Wisconsin, Department of Meteorology, page 18; © Lynn M. Stone all other photos

Title page: *The crew aboard the Space Shuttle Columbia tracked Hurricane Dolores, shown here in a view from space.*

Series Editor: Henry Rasof

Cover and interior design by Nicola Stratford

Library of Congress Cataloging-in-Publication Data

O'Hare, Ted, 1961-
  Studying weather / Ted O'Hare.
     v. cm. — (Weather report)
Contents: Studying weather — Studying climate — Meteorologists — Measuring weather — Weather stations — Weather instruments — Weather maps — Weather forecasters — Why study weather?
  ISBN 1-58952-573-6 (hardcover)
  1. Weather—Juvenile literature. 2. Meteorology—Juvenile literature. [1. Weather. 2. Meteorology.] I. Title. II. Series.
  QC981.3 .O39 2002
  551.5—dc21
                                        2002151637

Printed in the USA

CG/CG

Table of Contents

Studying weather

Weather is the word we use to tell us what it is like outside. The weather might be sunny, it might be hot, or it might be snowing. Weather helps people decide things. It helps them decide what to wear, what to do, and even what to grow.

People who study weather are called **meteorologists**. They need to learn about how weather works. And meteorologists need to know how to predict the weather.

Sunshine and a stiff breeze are good weather conditions for flying a kite on a Florida beach.

Studying climate

    Climate is the weather of a place over a period of time. Rainfall and temperatures are two of the things that make a place's climate.

    People keep records of climate. Scientists study these records. Because they study these records, scientists can tell if an area is good for growing certain crops. They also study records to look for changes in climate.

A dry climate shapes the way that plants and animals live in the desert.

Meteorologists

Benjamin Franklin was one of the founders of the United States. In the 1770s he also was one of the first people to study weather in North America.

Meteorologists today have special training and modern equipment. This helps them predict weather better than Franklin could. Today's meteorologists need to predict weather for the next day and for the future.

When it is sent into space, the modern GOES series of satellites help meteorologists forecast weather on earth.

Measuring weather

Meteorologists study and measure weather conditions. These scientists must measure the weight of the air. They must measure air temperature, ground temperature, and water temperature. They must also measure **humidity**, the amount of moisture in the air.

In addition, scientists need to measure wind speed and direction. And they measure **precipitation**, the amount of rain and snow that has fallen.

This thermometer in the Rockies shows that it is still winter!

Weather forecasts about storms like this help people avoid dangerous weather.

Signals from weather satellites are picked up by "dishes" at weather stations.

Weather stations

Weather stations are places where scientists gather information from **instruments**. These places can be found all over the world. Some weather stations float on oceans. Others are in buildings or on **satellites**. Weather satellites orbit through space. They send photos and information to stations on the ground.

An Atlas II/Centaur rocket blasts off with a weather satellite.

Weather instruments

Meteorologists use different sources to get information about weather. Some of these sources are satellites, computers, and radar. Scientists use an **anemometer** to measure wind speed.

You don't have to be a scientist to use some instruments. Anyone can use a **barometer**. This instrument measures the weight, or pressure, of air masses. A falling barometer shows that bad weather is on the way. A **thermometer** is used to measure air temperature. A rain gauge is used to measure the amount of rain.

Because winds are strong at this weather station on Mount Washington in New Hampshire, chains are used to hold the building in place.

THE HIGHEST WIND
EVER OBSERVED
BY MAN WAS
RECORDED HERE

231 MILES PER HOUR

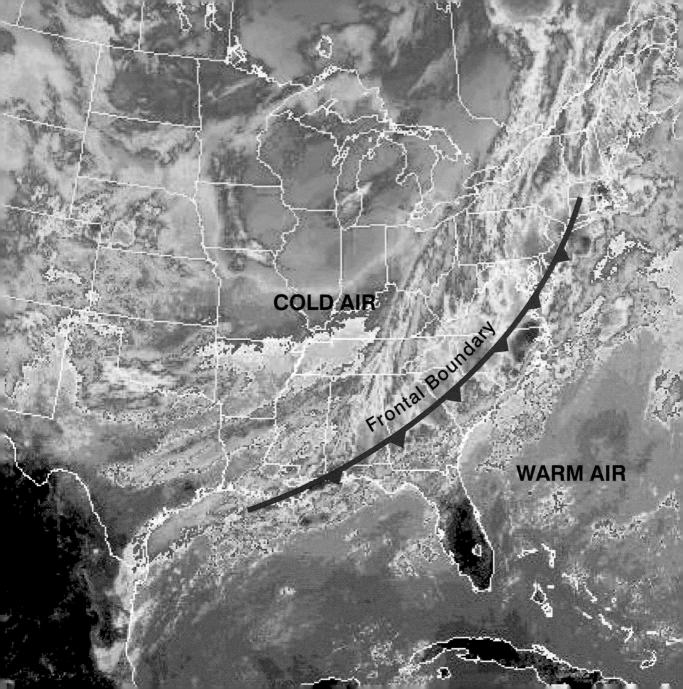

Weather maps

Weather maps help people see weather conditions. The maps show storms, temperatures, and where to find large weather systems known as **fronts**. A front is a boundary between masses of cold air and warmer air. As fronts move, weather in an area changes.

Weather maps help weather **forecasters** predict how the weather may change.

Computers print detailed weather maps from satellite signals.

Weather forecasters

Forecasters feed information about weather conditions into computers. Sometimes these are extremely fast and powerful computers called supercomputers. This information comes from instruments and from personal observation. The computer stores and processes information about the past and gathered from the present.

Computer operators in the Department of Meteorology at the University of Wisconsin gather weather information from all over the world.

Why study the weather?

By studying yesterday's weather, forecasters can often predict what tomorrow's weather—and weather of the future—will be like.

People study weather to find out if the earth's climate is changing. Is it really warmer in the world today than it was 100 years ago? Changing weather can have an impact on many people.

Glossary

anemometer (an uh MOM uh ter) — an instrument that measures wind speed

barometer (bar OHM uh ter) — an instrument that measures the pressure, or weight, of air

climate (KLY mut) — the type of weather conditions that a place has over a long period of time

forecasters (FOR kas terz) — people who predict things

fronts (FROHNTZ) — boundaries between two different masses of air

humidity (hu MID ih tee) — wetness or moisture in the air

instruments (IN struh mentz) — tools

meteorologists (mee tee uh ROL oh jistz) — people who study the weather

precipitation (pree sip uh TAY shun) — rain, snow, and sleet

satellites (SAT uh litez) — manmade weather stations

thermometer (thur MOM uh ter) — an instrument that measures temperature

weather (WEH thur) — what it is like outside on any day at any time

Index

Further Reading

Cosgrove, Brian. *Weather*. New York: Dorling Kindersley, 2000.

Gibbons, Gail. *Weather Forecasting*. New York: Four Winds, 1987.

Petty, Kate. *I Didn't Know That People Chase Twisters*. Brookfield, CT: Copper Beech, 1998.

Websites To Visit

www.miamisci.org/hurricane/weatherstation.html

www.nws.noaa.gov/om/educ/wxblarge.rm

www.usatoday.com/weather/wforcst0.htm

About The Author

Ted O'Hare is an author and editor of children's information books. He divides his time between New York City and a home upstate.

WITHDRAWN

Withdrawn